Mr. Welfare

A Play by Wendell Etherly

inkspil
inkspil.com

ISBN-13: 978-0983387770 (Inkspil Publishing)
ISBN-10: 098338777X

Writers Guild of America 150194

Wendell Etherly Mr. Welfare: a play in two acts

Characters

Joe – Black Male, Mid 30's, Tavern Owner

Kenny – Black Male, 21, Bartender

Mr. Rainey – Black Male, 60, Regular Customer

Leon – Black Male, Mid 30's, Regular Customer

Reginald – Black Male, Mid 50's, Indigent

Thomas – Black Male, Late 30's, Condescending, Business Consultant of Joe's

Rashied – Black Male, Late 20's, Young Muslim

Alderman Phillips – Black Male, Early 50's, Alderman of the Ward

Setting

The setting consists of a bar counter and four stools; four tables with two chairs a piece, and a jukebox that sits in the corner near the entrance.

We ask,
When will our struggle be no more?
When will our fight cease?
When will our tears dry up?
When will our goals be reached?

I say,
When your brother's needs become your own.
When your words become his strength.
When your shoulders lift his load.
When your choices consider his life.

-L.D. Etherly

Time:

Early 60's

Location:

Chicago, IL.

Act One

Scene One

A dim light comes up on an empty tavern. Kenny enters the bar from the back with beer mugs in hand. He lines them up across the back shelf behind the counter.

Joe: *[Offstage]* Kenny, come back here and get the rest of these mugs.

Kenny: Yes, sir. *[Kenny enters the back through the swing door. Moments later, Leon enters the bar. He walks over to the jukebox. Kenny enters from the back].* How many times Mr. Warren got to tell you that that jukebox ain't to be played before noon? You know he don't like that music on this early.

Leon: I ain't studin' that fool. I spend more money in here than anybody else. I got the right to play this here jukebox whenever I want. *[Leon puts his nickel in the machine. The music plays. Leon takes a seat at the bar].* Give me a Jack. *[Kenny makes the drink and places it in front of Leon].* You seen that line outside the office across the street?

Kenny: Yeah - look like the entire neighborhood out there.

Leon: Government must be giving more money these days. You know they ain't doing nothing but taking it from our pay. It ain't enough that we work hard to support ourselves, but on top of that we working to support lazy nigga's who don't wanna work, and single mothers we ain't never laid up with. Well, I ain't putting in forty plus hours a week so that the next man can get a free meal ticket – hell naw! I say, if a man don't wanna work let him starve, and if a family can't take care of their child give it to someone who can, simple as that.

Kenny: Well, I know a few of them people standing in that line, and all of them ain't lazy. Some working two – three jobs to make ends meet. I know some of them single mothers in that line, too, and I'm sure all of them didn't expect to be single. Some people just need a little help. Don't bother me none that the government take a little from my pay to help them out.

Leon: Damn all that! Ain't nobody taking care of me, and why should they? I'm willing and able to make my own living. Don't make no sense that we got to be responsible for folks that don't wanna take care of themselves. Every time I look at my check stub I see deductions from the union, the federal government, the state, and then something they call miscellaneous. Shouldn't be no miscellaneous on my check stub – I don't know nobody by that name. *[Joe enters from the back. He looks at Leon with a look of disgust. He walks over to the jukebox and pulls the plug from the wall].* What you go and do that for? I paid my nickel to listen to that song!

Joe: I done told you, Leon, I don't want that music playing in here before twelve o' clock.

Leon: Then what sense do it make having it sit there early in the morning if can't nobody play it till noon?

Joe: Ain't nobody gonna be pushing and pulling no damn jukebox out here everyday at noon cause your ass can't follow instruction. You ought'a be happy I open the bar this early to daytime-drunks like yourself. Now, I'm trying to run a respectable establishment here. All I ask is that you follow the rules like everybody else.

Leon: Fine, but you gonna give me my nickel back.

Joe reaches in his pocket and pulls out a nickel. He places it on the counter in front of Leon.

Jon: There's your nickel. Now I ain't gonna tell you no more about that jukebox.

Leon: *[Irritated]* Alright, man, I hear you!

Joe: Yeah, but is you listening? *[Kenny walks over to the window].* That line gone down any?

Kenny: Ain't no way of telling. I still can't see the end of it.

Joe: That office been opened for a little over an hour. You'd think everybody be able to fit in there by now.

Kenny walks behind the bar counter.

Leon: That line is wrapped all the way around 79th street – them folks ain't getting in there. Office be closed before the end of the line reach the corner.

Joe: Well, they need to hire some more help over there. It may get folks in and out faster.

Leon: All this time folks spend standing in that line, they could've been out looking for work.

Rashied enters.

Rashied: Al-salaamu alaykum, brotha's!

Joe: *[Playfully]* And a salami on rye to you too, Rashied!

Rashied: Very funny, brotha. I'm glad to see you're in good spirits this morning.

Leon: What you doing up in here? Don't Allah got restrictions on places like these?

Rashied: The Honorable Elijah Muhammad teaches us that we must go wherever the truth is needed, and the truth is surely needed in a place like this.

Joe: Alright now, don't you bring that "Honorable Elijah Muhammad" nonsense up in here. Contrary to what you Muslims may believe, this here is a place of refuge, a place where folks come to unwind. Now, if you wanna go outside, and preferably across the street, then you go ahead. I'm sure them folks can use a good word of encouragement. You can go over there and preach till you blue in the face. Hell, preach until it's your final call, I don't care, but don't bring that up in here.

Kenny enters from the back.

Kenny: Hey, Rashied.

Rashied: Hey, brotha.

Kenny: I hear Malcolm X is speaking at the mosque next week. That true?

Rashied: That's right, brotha!

Kenny: Man, I've been wanting to hear him speak for some time now. I've heard him on the radio plenty, but never in person.

Rashied: Dynamic speaker, isn't he?

Kenny: Yeah, he something else.

Rashied: Believe it or not, Brother Malcolm used to be a two bit hustler before he learned the truth.

Leon: And I bet ain't much changed.

Rashied: Don't let a man's troubled past compel you to judgment, brotha. The Minister Malcolm is no fluke. He's truly anointed by Allah, and appointed by the Honorable Elijah Muhammad.

Joe: And what the hell is that supposed to mean? I know plenty of crooked ministers who preach fire and brimstone undoubtedly knowing they're headed there themselves.

Rashied: Well, I can't speak for all ministers, but I can most definitely vouch for the Minister Malcolm X. In fact, I can vouch for all of whom I know within the Nation of Islam. And you'd be surprised of what some of our brothers and sisters have overcome. But that goes to show that the renewal of the mind and spirit is a beautiful thing.

Kenny: What you mean, the renewal of the mind and spirit?

Rashied: It means to be transformed; to turn from your wicked ways and embrace a whole new way of life. You see, when a man finds revelation of the truth it's like a battle takes place within himself. And as the inner man begins to change, so does the outer man.
That's what we call a conversion.

Joe: Sounds more like what the Catholics call an exorcism.

Rashied: Call it what you will, but through conversion you find deliverance. But as I said, that only comes through revelation.

Kenny: And Revelation comes through truth.

Rashied: That's right, brotha. The Honorable Elijah Muhammad teaches us how to be better men, better husbands, and better providers for our families.

Joe: And what make you think he got all the right answers? He ain't nothing but a man just like you. What make him qualified enough to teach you to be a better provider?

Rashied: Because the Honorable Elijah Muhammad possesses a wealth of knowledge, and his teachings have brought about great results. Take a look outside that window there. I bet you won't find not one faithful Muslim in that line across the street. You know why? It's because we've been educated. We've been taught to take care of ourselves and not to rely on a government that would rather have us neutralized and vanished from the face of the earth.

Mr. Rainey enters.

Joe: *[Pleasantly]* Well, good morning, Mr. Rainey.

Rainey: Good morning, Joseph - fella's.

10

Kenny: Good morning, Mr. Rainey.

Joe: Ain't that line out there something?

Rainey: Something awful. Look like the great depression all over again, except it ain't affecting nobody but black folks.

Rainey sits down at the bar.

Kenny: What can I get you this morning?

Rainey: Same old – coffee no cream.

Kenny: Yes, sir.

Rainey: So what's the dispute this morning?

Joe: This fool here talking about how the government wanna do away with us - rid the world of black folks. But I'm trying to tell him that ain't nobody capable of such things but God himself

Rashied: I'm not talking about removing the very presence of black people. I'm talking about a state of conditioning that would cause us to believe that we have no purpose in this life. And there's no difference between that and extinction. It's been a little over two hundred years since Willie Lynch delivered his speech on the bank of the James River, and to this day his methods still apply to people of color all over this country.

Rainey: That's that slave owner fella, isn't it?

Rashied: That's right. In fact, the term "lynching" derived from his name. He traveled to several plantations to teach his methods to other slave owners.

Kenny: What kind'a methods?

Rashied: Methods of fear – distrust; *[he points at Kenny and Joe]* turning the young black male against the older black male - *[then pointing to Joe*

and Leon] the dark skin slave against the light skin slave – the black male against the black female, and so forth. And that method alone has caused black women of today to rely on themselves rather than the black man, and that shouldn't be. Allah has called the man to be the priest, provider and protector of his household. Women shouldn't have to bear that burden as well as their own.

Joe: So you really believe that something a white man said two hundred years ago still got a hold on black people today?

Rashied: That's right, brotha.

Joe: Man, ya'll some of the most superstitious nigga's I've ever met. If you ask me, ya'll the ones who suffering from conditioning. I mean, what man in his right mind believe in such things? If white folks heard the way you was talking it's liable you'd be committed.

Rashied: I know it may sound crazy to you, but Willie Lynch understood that the mind is the most vital instrument of a man, and if you can control that you can control the man behind it. And if his methods had been installed correctly it would control the slave for at least three hundred years. It's only been two hundred and forty years since that day. According to Willie Lynch, we still got another sixty years of conditioning to go. That's a whole new millennium, brotha's. But we can't afford that. That's why it's important that our minds be renewed.

Kenny: That's some heavy stuff, Rashied. Where you learn all that?

Rashied: Through some of the classes that the Nation of Islam provides to aspired ministers and teachers. If you're interested there's a class every Thursday evening at the center. It's open to the public. Why don't you come by and listen to some of the teachings.

Kenny: I don't know about all that, Rashied. I mean, I got my god and you got yours. I ain't trying to be transformed or nothing like that. I just like to hear a good black message from time to time. I'll take one of those fliers though.

Rashied hands Kenny a flier.

Rashied: May Allah bless you real good. And maybe after the service you can come back and share some SOUND doctrine with these brotha's here.

Leon: Shit, he ain't gonna find no sound doctrine amongst you Muslims. Walking around here screaming Allah this, Allah that, Elijah this, Muhammad that. How you expect a man to switch sides when all his life he been taught that Jesus saves. Ain't nobody familiar with no 'Allah'. I ain't never even heard a song about Allah. Least ya'll can do is write a song so we know who Allah is.

Joe: Sho' nough.

Leon: And don't no black man wanna hear that pork ain't good for the body. You asking him to roll over and drop dead when you tell him something like that. Hell, pork is half a nigga's nourishment.

Rashied: And that's why so many black men and women are dying before their time; because they don't want to give up things that are harmful to their bodies. If you brotha's knew how filthy the pig is maybe you'd think differently.

Leon: I know how filthy it is. You ain't even got to cut it open to see it ain't the cleanest animal; the way it be running around and rolling in the mud, snorting and carrying on, anybody can see it ain't clean. But hell, a mule walk through the field and shit on crops all day long, you ain't talking bout how fruits and vegetables are harmful to the body.

Rashied: Fruits and vegetables are cleaned and sterilized thoroughly.

Leon: I clean my meat – I clean it real good. Then when it come time to eat I pray over it. But then again we don't talk to the same god so I don't know how it work for your people. But the God I been raised to know say I can bless my food and it be cleansed. Now, if Allah can't do the same you ought'a find you a new god, cause that's a pitiful excuse for a god.

Joe: Sho' nough is. I mean, an ordinary man can clean a filthy piece of meat well enough to eat it. Now if a god can't do the same you got to go back and think about some things; like how could you serve a god that can't purify your meat better than you can.

Rainey: Now, ya'll leave the young man alone. Ain't nothing wrong with him believing in such things. At least he believe in something. That's more than I can say about most folks these days. The world done beat us down so to the point where we don't believe in nothing anymore, not even the God we been raised to know. Guess we been serving everybody else for so long we figure when it come time to be free we ain't serving nobody else. Sounds legitimate, yes, but it's sad cause it be the death of us. Son, you go ahead and blow your horn as much as you'd like.

Rashied: Thank you, Mr. Rainey. Say, would you like to attend next weeks service? It's open to all the public. The Honorable Elijah Muhammad has always…

Rainey: Now, son, just because I say blow your horn don't mean I'm interested in the tune.

Rashied: I understand. What about you, Joe?

Joe: I ain't in to that kind'a thing.

Rashied: Leon? *[Leon looks in the other direction].* Well, I bid you brotha's fare well. *[To Kenny]* And I'll see you next week.

Kenny: Sure thing.

Rashied: Well, take care.

Rainey: Bye.

Rashied exits.

Joe: Give me this! *[Joe snatches the flier from Kenny's hand].* What the hell you doing asking for one of these fliers? You ain't no Muslim.

Kenny: You don't have to be no Muslim to attend the service. Its open to all the public, anybody can go.

Joe: Why you wanna go and let them fill your head with all that foolishness?

Kenny: It ain't nothing foolish. They just be talking about the state of our people.

Joe: If I didn't know any better, I'd think you been before.

Kenny: I have. I attended a service last year, and it was something else. Ya'll ought'a go and see for yourselves. You wouldn't be out of place. All sorts of folks attend, even Christians.

Joe: Well, you ain't gonna be there this year, cause I'm gonna make sure I schedule you to work that morning.

Kenny: The tavern ain't open on Sundays.

Joe: It will be that Sunday. If Christians double-minded enough to attend a Muslim service, then I'm gonna be like-minded and open the tavern on the Lords day.

Leon: Make sense to me.

Kenny: I just wanted to go hear Malcolm X.

Joe: I don't give a damn! If you go to that service you gonna be out of a job, you hear?

Pause

Kenny: Yes, sir.

Joe: Now go on back there and clean the rest of those mugs. *[Kenny exits to the back]*. I don't know what's wrong with folks these days. Seem like they motivated by most anything now. A minister call the white man a devil and folks standing in line to hear what he gonna say next. And what for? He ain't nothing but a racist preacher with a bad attitude.

Rainey: That may be so, but our people need to hear this kind'a message right now. May not be but for a season or so, but we need to hear it. Got to embrace it while it's here cause there'll come a time when you be wanting to hear something like it and can't find it cause somebody done away with it.

Leon: And you know they will.

Joe: So how you been, Mr. Rainey? We ain't seen you around here lately.

Rainey: That's because I've been in Georgia for the last few weeks.

Joe: Oh yeah?

Rainey: Uh huh.

Joe: You got family down there, I reckon?

Rainey: Yep. I'm the only one out of all of us to leave the south.

Joe: Well, I can't say I blame you with all that's been going on down there. Just the other day I seen a photo of a woman being hosed down in the middle of the street like she was in flames.

Rainey: Yeah, they keeping up a lot of trouble down there. But it was even worse when I was coming up.

Leon: Is that why you come up here – to get away from that ass whipping them white folks giving down there?

Rainey: Nah, I come up here for an adventure. I got tired of that country living - wanted something different.

Joe: Well, did you find what you was looking for?

Rainey: Sure did. Got into a heap of trouble when I got up here too.

Kenny: What kind'a trouble, Mr. Rainey?

Rainey: I met me a woman - a gorgeous woman.

Joe: Yeah?

Rainey: Yep. I met her at the bus station. It was fifteen minutes after I stepped foot on Illinois soil. And there she was sitting on the bench, waiting for the next city bus to arrive. So I introduced myself expecting she'd do the same. And do you think she did? Hell naw! That woman cut her eyes and looked in the other direction. I thought to myself, if all city folks like this woman here maybe I ought'a take my country ass back home. Well, after a while of sitting there in silence she asked me where I was from. When I told her I was a native of Georgia she started to warm up to me some. Come to find out she was from the country herself. Then we got to talking about some of everything; her family, her job, the city – we talked for hours. Wasn't too long before she suggested I come to her place and stay the evening, seeing as it was getting dark and I had no place to go. So later on when we finally got to her apartment she cooked me a hot meal and ran me a hot bath, just treating me like she known me for years. And when it was time to go to sleep she even insisted that I sleep in her bed – with her. Now, I just met this girl, mind you. I wasn't prepared to be sleeping with her. But who was I to argue? I wasn't gonna oppose it, she was beautiful.

Joe: So did you lay that pipe?

Rainey: All night long! And believe it or not, I turned out to be her first.

Leon: Now you a fool to believe you that woman's first. Any woman that's that hot between the legs done had her share of men. Ain't no respectable woman gonna let a man get between her legs in a few hours time.

Rainey: I ain't said nothing about her being respectable. I said I was her first. Ya see, I was laying the pipe for a whole week until guess who walked in?

Joe: Her man.

Rainey: Nope.

Kenny: Her mama?

Rainey: Nope.

Joe: Who then?

Rainey: Her *woman*.

Joe: Her woman?

Leon: What you talking about, her woman?

Rainey: Just like I said – her woman. She turned out to be a bull dagger.

Joe: You kidding!

Rainey: I kid you not. She had never even been with a man.

Leon: Man, get the hell out of here!

Rainey: I ain't lying. She was as bull dagger as I am home-grown. And her woman was ugly as an ape and big as a buck. I mean, she was something unnatural looking – creature like. And she was tall as a Goliath and heavy as a bear. But she was light on her feet, ya see, cause we didn't hear her when she walked in the house.

Joe: What she do when she find you in bed with her girl?

Rainey: She put a rifle to the back of my head and told me to turn around so that she could get a good look at me. Man, I tell you, I was terrified. I had never in my life seen nothing to the likes of her. I mean, that woman looked like she could eat me alive if I was seasoned properly. I said, "I'm a friend of your daughters, ma'am". She said, "that ain't my daughter, fool – that's my woman!" Boy, I jumped out of that bed so fast you'da thought it was on fire. I said, "she ain't tell me she had a woman." The girl looked at the woman and said, "I did to tell him! He forced himself on me!"

Joe: Damn! How you get out of that one?

Rainey: Well, when I saw that begging for my life wasn't gonna work, I figured I had a better chance of fighting my way out. So I got her on the ground and took off for the door.

Kenny: So you got away?

Rainey: Yeah, but not without paying the price. She got me right here in the back of my shoulder. Funny thing is I didn't even know it until I stopped running.

Joe: Is that right?

Rainey: Yes, sir. Doctor said if the bullet would've come any closer to my heart I'da died.

Joe: So was it all worth leaving your home in Georgia?

Rainey: Well, I did find me the adventure I was looking for. And I eventually met me a good woman – got me a good job. I'd say it was.

Leon: Hell, you could'a found all that in Georgia, especially a good woman. I hear country women is the best women to have. I hear they'll cook for you, clean for you, give you good loving, and don't mind if you got two or three women on the side.

Rainey: And most of that is all true about a country woman, but I don't know who done told you that they don't mind a man having two or three women on the side. Hell, they kill you for that. And get away with it too.

Joe: Tell'em, Mr. Rainey.

Rainey: The country got a lot of empty land, not to mention a lot of distance between your house and the neighbors. Your woman'll kill you at ten o' clock in the p.m. and have you buried in the front yard by twelve in the a.m., and nobody be around for miles to witness a thing. But then again, country women have always been known as virtuous women. As long as their households were in order they didn't mind too much of nothing. But that was years ago, see. And since then they done learned how to interpret them scriptures well enough to know that submitting to your husband don't mean letting him do whatever he want to do.

Joe: It sho' don't. Hell, some of them delivering the sermon on Sunday mornings.

Rainey: That's right! The woman ain't taking the back end to a man no more, and they less tolerable of his nonsense. Now, there was a time when a woman let you hit her and sleep around on her, treat her any kind of way and she'd still keep a smile on her face when she see you walk through the door. But now the tables done turned, see. Women know how to play the game too, and they play it a whole lot better than a man. These women out here now will two time you and you'll never know it unless she tell you.

Joe: That's right. And more than likely you may never find out cause women got sense enough to take it to the grave. I know my ex-wife taking a mouth full with her.

Kenny: I never knew you were married before, Mr. Warren.

Joe: Sure was, and I was just a little younger than you. I married her right out of high school. We thought we were in love. But I didn't know any better. I didn't think about all the provisions that were necessary to take care of a woman. I just thought love would see us through. Oh, but Vickie made it quite clear that love had to be accompanied by wealth. And that woman made me aware of that in the most disrespectful manner. It got so bad between us that I nearly put my hands on her.

Kenny: You wasn't hitting her were you, Mr. Warren?

Joe: Nah, she left long before it got to that point. But if I had known what

I know now, I sure would have waited.

Rainey: Well, let me be on my way. Thanks for the coffee, Joseph.

Joe: Anytime, Mr. Rainey. It's always a pleasure talking with you. Hey, maybe I'll see you in the morning.

Rainey: I don't know about tomorrow morning, but I'll sure be here tomorrow evening to hear Muddy Waters.

Joe: Alright. I'll see you tomorrow evening then.

Rainey: Ya'll have a good day.

Joe: You, too, Mr. Rainey. *[Rainey exits].* Old man got a lot of wisdom, don't he? And some funny stories, I tell you.

Leon: Muddy Waters supposed to be here tomorrow night?

Joe: Yep.

Leon: How come I didn't know?

Joe: Cause you ain't read the sign before you walked in here. It's right on the window near the front door – been up there for a whole week.

Leon: Damn! I sho' wish I'd known sooner.

Joe: Why? Ain't like you gonna miss it – you here every day.

Leon: I've been trying to get this young gal out, but by time I get around to ask her to go somewhere she make other plans.

Joe: Well, you still ought'a ask. I'm sure once you tell her that Muddy Waters gonna be here she'll cancel whatever plans she do got – just give her a call.

Leon: Yeah, maybe I will. Who can resist Muddy Waters?

Joe: Nobody I know.

The phone rings. Kenny answers.

Kenny: *[On the phone]* Joe's Tavern. Oh, hey, Mr. Fleming. Uh huh – uh huh, sure thing, I'll tell him. *[Kenny hangs up the phone]. [To Joe]* Mr. Fleming says he'll be here in a few hours to drop off some forms.

Leon: You still working with that uppity nigga?

Joe: You damn right I am! He got ideas that'll help raise my property value a full seventy five percent.

Leon: You keep him around and he gonna run away the little business you do have.

Joe: How you figure that? His ideas have raised the property value of a lot of real estate around here. First thing the alderman say after I purchased this building was to call Thomas Fleming cause he can raise its value by three times. And since working with him, I've seen business increase by twenty percent already. Hell, uppity he may be, but he sure as hell know what he doing.

Leon: Well, real estate may be his profession, but this a different place than where he come from. People like things plain and simple around here. If a man wanna play the jukebox, he ought'a be able to come in here and play it at any hour with no restrictions. This here is a tavern, not a bistro.

Joe: Well, if a few rules gonna keep nigga's from coming in here to drink then so be it. I don't want that kind'a element in here no ways. If you wanna be unruly, take your ass to Theresa's Lounge. That hole in a wall can accommodate such foolishness, but not Joe's Tavern, no sir! I'm trying to establish something different here – something better. And if ever it start to looking like this place is becoming something it shouldn't, I'll destroy it myself. And I mean that. If anybody gonna destroy this muthafucka, it's gonna be me.

Leon: So what Thomas charging you for his services anyway?

Joe: A mere ten percent of my profit.

Leon: That *mere* ten percent gonna eventually add up.

Joe: Just as long as the business keep growing, it's fine by me.

Pause

Leon: Well, I guess I'd better get on to work.

Joe: *[Playfully]* I'm surprised you function well enough to keep a job as much time as you spend in here drinking.

Leon: Don't you be worrying about how much time I spend in here. My time belong to me, not you.

Joe: I ain't said I was worried about how much time you spend in here, I can care less. Hell, you the one keep my mortgage paid every month. I just wonder how you function well enough to keep a job.

Leon: It's the liquor that keep me running. Can't work without it, can't go home without it. It's like gasoline.

Joe: *[Playfully]* Well, ain't no sense in me telling you to slow down cause you wouldn't listen.

Leon: Nah, ain't no sense in telling me that cause you don't care. Like you say, I'm your best customer. Why would you care about how much time I spend in here drinking? Long as you get your money before I leave, all is right with the world. *[Leon places his money on the top of the bar]*. I'll see you this evening.

Joe: Alright.

Leon exits. Kenny enters from the back.

Kenny: Leon gone already?

Joe: Yeah, he just left.

Kenny: Boy, he sho' got a high tolerance for that liquor. He had five Jacks in a half hour. I mean, I ain't known him that long, but it seem like he got some problems.

Joe: Who ain't these days?

Kenny: Yeah, but I don't know many who be drinking like him this early in the morning.

Joe: Well, what good do it do me to prevent a drunk from fueling up? Hell, this is a business!

The lights go down.

Scene Two

The lights come up on the tavern. It's later that afternoon. Kenny is behind the bar counter reading a newspaper. Joe enters from the back.

Joe: *[Sarcastically]* What's that you reading, "Muhammad Speaks"?

Kenny: Nah, it's the Defender. I'm reading this article about how the military affects the behavior of black men, and how they ain't never the same when they return home.

Joe: Well, it ain't only black men that's affected by it. War changes the demeanor of any man. It just ain't natural to see some of the things you see when you in the line of fire. And I'm sure them boys heading to Vietnam gonna be even worse off when they return.

Kenny: Says here that most military vets come home with bad addictions. You come home with any bad habits, Mr. Warren?

Joe: None that I know of. I ain't doing nothing now that I wasn't doing before I enlisted. But like I said, this is a different war – different stakes, and when it's all said and done ain't many returning home at all.

Kenny: I heard Leon say he served in the military years ago too. You think that got anything to do with him drinking so much?

Joe: Could be. I don't know what he's seen. We ain't never talked about it, but then none of us vets do. A lot of us done seen some things that we'd rather not reflect on. When you come home from the military the best thing to do is leave those memories in the jungle, or wherever you served, and set your mind on something good – like a career and a family.

Kenny: I remember asking Leon if he had a family once, but he didn't have much to say.

Joe: As far as I know, his wife left him shortly after he returned home; took his two girls with her too.

Kenny: Well, that would explain why he didn't wanna talk about it.

Joe: Did you wipe those tables down yet?

Kenny: Yes sir, a little while ago.

Joe: Well, why don't you go on and take your lunch. I got some sandwiches back there.

Kenny: Okay.

Kenny exits to the back. Joe walks over to the jukebox. He puts a nickel in and selects a song. The music plays. Joe walks back over to the bar. Alderman Phillips enters.

Phillips: Joseph Warren.

Joe: *[Excited]* Alderman Phillips. What you doing in here, man! Come on here and sit down. *[Phillips sits down at the bar]*. How you been?

Phillips: Fine, and you?

Joe: Oh, I've been alright.

Phillips: I see you got the place looking nice.

Joe: Yeah, but I still got a lot more work to do to it. Can I get you something?

Phillips: Give me a bourbon.

Joe: Sure. *[Joe makes the drink].* Here you go.

Phillips: Thank you.

Joe: So, what brings you around here? I mean, I know this is your Ward and all, but it ain't everyday you see the alderman walking down the street, let alone in a tavern ordering a drink.

Phillips: I had to take care of some things around here. I've been getting complaints from public aid recipients about the office across the street. They're saying that the workers aren't getting folks in and out fast enough.

Joe: I always thought they mailed them checks out.

Phillips: They do, but those people in line are new registries'.

Joe: Well, them lines been so long, everybody ain't been able to get in there before the office close. I wouldn't blame it on the workers though. They couldn't help all of them people in a day if they wanted to. And you know how folks are when it come to their aid.

Phillips: Well, I pray for the day when folks ain't got to rely on government assistance anymore. It's become a handicap in our communities. Won't nobody want to work as long as they see an opportunity to get by. Hell, if it were up to me I'd cut it all together. I know that may sound kind'a harsh, but it would sho' make folks go out and find work.

Joe: I agree. But everybody out there ain't trying to get by. Some of those folks just need a little help until they can get back on their feet.

Phillips: Yeah, but how do you weed them out from those who are taking advantage of it – there's no way of knowing. Now, I'm sure when Roosevelt felt necessary to provide government assistance it was with the best of intentions. But when it became the root of our sustenance it became a cancer in our community's.

Joe: So what you gonna do about them long lines across the street?

Phillips: Nothing. Folks just gonna have to go to some of the other offices in the city. If they need government assistance that bad they'll have to travel for it.

Joe: Man, I tell you, times are hard. The minute you think you got it all figured out they up and change the rules on you.

Phillips: Yeah, it's a shame. Even most of the shelters in the city are full. You'd think they'd be empty seeing as it's the summer. Most homeless folks don't mind sleeping on the street in this type of weather, but that's just how many homeless people we got in this community. *[Pause]* Listen, Joseph, I need your help.

Joe: Sure.

Phillips: You got any empty rooms for rent?

Joe: Yeah, but I didn't wanna start renting them to nobody until I did some more work to them. Why you ask?

Phillips: Because there's about six older citizens I know that need somewhere to stay for a little while. I ain't looking for nothing fancy, just somewhere they can lay their heads.

Joe: Now, I don't know about that. I mean, I respect what you trying to do and all, but the only folks I want occupying them rooms are tenants who can afford to pay rent.

Phillips: That wouldn't be a problem.

Joe: How come it wouldn't? They wouldn't be living on the streets if they could afford to take on rent.

Phillips: What I mean is – I intend to cover the expense.

Joe: You?

Phillips: Yes.

Joe: And how long would they need to stay?

Phillips: Maybe two – three months at the most. I can use the money from my Ward's budget to cover the rent. So, what do you say?

Pause

Joe: I don't know, Alderman Phillips. I got folks looking to move in as soon as I get things together.

Phillips: It's only temporary. Won't be but for a couple months or so, and I'll pay you fifty dollars more than what you're asking for. Just do me this one favor, Joseph, and I won't forget it.

Joe: Even if I did decide to rent to them how they gonna eat? I can't feed them.

Phillips: I already paid Estella to provide three meals a day for them. She just needs to know where to deliver the meals. *[Pause]* Can I give her this address?

Pause

Joe: Alright, but only for two months. I got to get the place ready for the new tenants.

Phillips: How much?

Joe: Fifty dollars a month.

Phillips: Good. I'll give you a hundred dollars a month for each person. I'll write you a check to cover both months.

Joe: Oh, ain't no need for you to do that right now. I know you're good for it.

Phillips: I just want to show my gratitude. *[Alderman Phillips pulls out his checkbook and writes a check].* I really appreciate you doing this, Joseph. You're doing a great service for your community. *[Alderman Phillips rips the check from the checkbook and hands it to Joseph].* Here you go.

Joe: *[Reading the check]* "The City Council of Chicago". And you sure this ain't too much at one time?

Phillips: Not at all. I just want to see to it that these people are taken care of. I'll send them over here first thing in the morning, say around eight o' clock?

Joe: Eight o' clock is fine.

Phillips: Good, and thanks for the drink.

Joe: You're welcome.

Phillips: I'll talk to you soon.

Joe: Alright.

Alderman Phillips exits. Kenny enters.

Kenny: Who was that, Mr. Warren?

Joe: It was Alderman Phillips.

Kenny: No kidding?

Joe: Nah.

Kenny: What he come here for?

Joe: Damn, boy, why you ask so many questions? Ain't none of your business why he come here. Get over there and clean them tables off. We got to get ready for the evening rush.

Kenny: Yes, sir.

Joe exits to the back. Kenny cleans the tables. Thomas enters.

Thomas: Hey, Kenny.

Kenny: Hey there, Mr. Fleming.

Thomas: Is Joe around?

Kenny: Yeah, he's in the back. *[Calling out]* Hey, Mr. Warren, Mr. Fleming is here to see you.

Joe: *[From backstage]* I'll be up there in a minute.

Thomas takes a seat at the bar counter.

Thomas: Preparing for a rush, huh?

Kenny: Yeah, it tend to get busy around this time. Can I get you something to drink?

Thomas: A glass of water if you will. *[Kenny pours Thomas a glass of water]*. Thank you.

Kenny: Uh huh.

Kenny pulls the newspaper from under the bar and returns to reading it.

Thomas: You know, I always wondered why a smart young man like yourself would be working in a place like this.

Kenny: Money don't come much easier than it do in here. All I do is pour drinks throughout the day.

Thomas: Yeah, but there's so much more you could be doing with your life.

Kenny: Like what?

Thomas: Have you ever considered going to college?

Kenny: *[Chuckles]* College? I ain't cut out for no college.

Thomas: And what makes you say that?

Kenny: Cause I barely got out of high school. How I look applying to somebody's college? Besides, it wouldn't do me no good anyhow. I need to earn me a living now.

Thomas: I understand. But it's important to know that education is the only way a black man can find true success in this world.

Kenny: What about Mr. Warren? He ain't got no college degree and he doing pretty well for himself.

Thomas: Joe would be the first to tell you, it wasn't nothing but luck that got him this building. Alderman Phillips saw that he was in need so he sold it to him for little of nothing. Joe opened a tavern because he figured as long as men were having problems they would always be drinking, and that alone was his business plan. But truth is, the only thing he really does is manage this place. I'm the one who owns it. He wouldn't know the difference though.

Kenny: How you figure you own it when he's the one who bought the building?

Thomas: Anytime a man knows how much money you make before you do shows that he has ownership. Yeah, it's his business. His name is on the lease. He makes all the decisions. But I'm the one who has access to all the money. I'm the one reporting to the IRS every month. I'm the one filling out all sorts of forms that he don't bother reading because he doesn't understand them. I ask him to sign the forms, so he signs them. But does he know what he's signing? No. He's got to trust that I'm not going to run off one day and take all that he has. Now, if I'm uncomfortable with that arrangement, I'm sure it doesn't sit well with him. That's why I say go to college. That way you can manage your business as well as own it.

Kenny: I ain't never thought about it that way.

Thomas: Well, you'd better start, especially if you intend to live comfortably.

Kenny: How long did it take you to get through college?

Thomas: Four years to obtain my Bachelors Degree.

Kenny: Four years? That's a long time, Mr. Fleming.

Thomas: But it's well worth it. And when you think about it four years really isn't all that bad. By time you arrive there and get deep into your studies it'll be time for you to come back home. And you'll see that nothing really changed. Everything will be just the way you left it. .

Kenny: Yeah, but what about my mama? It's only me and her.

Thomas: You don't have to go away to school. There's several colleges right here in the state of Illinois.

Kenny: What about Bernadette? She ain't gonna like the idea of me leaving my job to attend school. She wanna be married soon.

Thomas: Well, you'd better tell Bernadette to slow down some. Tell her you have other things you want to do first. And if she can't understand that then you may have to let her go for the time being. I understand you love this young lady and all, but you have to do what's best for you. Marriage isn't going anywhere. It's been here since the beginning of time. It'll be here when you get back. And it'll be a whole lot sweeter when you're capable of taking care of her.

Kenny: I don't know if I can make Bernadette see it that way. She having a hard enough time accepting that I work in a tavern. But I do know she'll tolerate me serving liquor before she'll allow me to leave this job to attend college.

Joe enters.

Joe: You got here right in time. *[Joe hands Thomas the check]*. Take a look at that.

Thomas: What is it?

Joe: It's a check, fool – what it look like?

Thomas: Yeah, but from where?

Joe: Alderman Phillips.

Thomas: I don't understand. Why would Alderman Phillips write you a check for twelve hundred dollars?

Kenny: *[Surprised]* Alderman Phillips wrote you a check for twelve hundred dollars? That's a lot of money, Mr. Warren.

Thomas: It sure is. That's why I'm concerned.

Joe: Now, there you go with that skepticism. Ain't nothing to be concerned about. He asked me to rent my apartments to a few of the older citizens in the community; six of'em total. And they only gonna be here for two months. I didn't see any problem with it, so I agreed to it. And he paid me in advance – a hundred dollars a month for each person; fifty dollars more than I asked for.

Thomas: What about the families we had lined up to move in next month?

Joe: You got a twelve hundred dollar check in your hand. Those folks can wait an extra month before they move in.

Thomas: But they're planning to move in next month.

Joe: Then they just gonna have to wait. Tell them I got a few more things to do to the building before they move in. It'll be ready for them in another month.

Thomas: But these are good people, Joseph. People who are going to take good care of your building and pay their rent on time. We don't want to disappoint them.

Joe: *You* don't want to disappoint them. I can care less. I ain't no respecter of money. Rent money is rent money, don't matter who's hand it come from. I ain't never heard of nothing that say good people give better money. Hell, if a dollar roll out of a man's ass I'm gonna open the register and put it in there with the others. Besides, now we got money we wasn't expecting to have. That twelve hundred dollars can come in handy.

Thomas: But the plan was to rent out every apartment by the end of the summer.

Joe: And we will. These folks only gonna be here for two months. After they leave the others can move in.

Thomas: Who's to say these people don't leave in two months?

Joe: Two months is what me and Alderman Phillips agreed to. That's what he paid me for.

Thomas: Did you get it in writing?

Joe: Nah, wasn't no need for all that.

Thomas: Joseph, you can't make these kinds of decisions within minutes. You have to take time to think about what you're doing. Just because a man offers you fifty dollars more than what you're asking for doesn't mean you take the money. You don't know what kind of people the alderman has you providing shelter for. You could be harboring escaped convicts for all you know.

Joe: They ain't no damn convicts! They're homeless citizens. They ain't got nowhere else to go, and since I got the resources to help them that's what I done.

Thomas: It would have been helpful had you allowed them to stay for a few days. A week would've been more than enough time for the alderman to find something else. But now you've over extended yourself. You might as well call these people tenants.

Joe: Look, Alderman Phillips said they wouldn't be here no longer than two months. Now, I ain't got a problem with that. And how I look telling the alderman that I couldn't help him anyway? He the reason I got this building in the first place. Now, if I thought it would be harmful to me, or the business I wouldn't have gone along with it. But the only thing the alderman trying to do is help these folks get off the street. And that check he wrote was enough to convince me of that.

Thomas: Why do you go out of your way to undermine my efforts?

Joe: What you talking about?

Thomas: A year ago, when I decided that I was going to help you strengthen this establishment, against my better judgment, if I might add, we agreed that every decision would be made by the both of us. But every time I turn around you go and do something that causes a setback in our original plans.

Joe: And I promise you there won't be any more delays from here on out.

Pause

Thomas: Alright – alright. But if it happens again I'm going to have to walk away for good. So for the time being, if you want to risk losing good tenants over this agreement you made with the alderman, that's your prerogative. But when things start to get out of hand, and them bums start to run amuck, don't call me.

Joe: Ain't gonna be nobody running amuck in my building, so don't you worry about that. You just go deposit that check – that's what you go do.

Thomas surrenders.

Thomas: Alright. I need you to sign all of those tax forms. I'm going to come by tomorrow to pick them up. We have to mail them off first thing in the morning. *[To Kenny]* And you think about what I said.

Thomas exits.

Joe: The nerve of him, coming up in here trying to tell me who I should rent to and who I
shouldn't.

Kenny: You can't expect him to understand, Mr. Warren. He don't even live around these parts. He just pass through twice a week to drop off them business forms. He don't know nothing about the folks who live in this community.

Joe: Yeah, but he ain't no fool either.

Kenny: Well, I think you doing a good thing by letting them stay here. You
helping the homeless and you getting paid for it. Don't get much better than that.

Joe: I guess it don't.

Kenny: Say, Mr. Warren, what you think about me going to college?

Joe: I don't know. Is that what you wanna do?

Kenny: I ain't never been too interested in it before until Mr. Fleming brought it up.

Joe: Guess it depends on the profession you wanna go into. I never thought it was something you'd ever need though.

Kenny: Me either. I had always planned to become a barber. Buy me a building - open a barbershop and run my business from the ground floor, just like you doing.

Joe: Then I don't see why it would be necessary to pay all that tuition for something you don't need. Not that I oppose it, but college is for more of a high level profession like medicine or law. Otherwise, it won't make you no more qualified than a man who prefers to learn *on* the job.

Kenny: That's the way I see it. And the experience of learning on the job prepares a man a whole lot better than any classroom ever could. What sense would it make to go to college for four years when I can spend that time working in my field. Hell, at this rate I'll be four years more qualified than the fella who goes to college.

Joe: That's right! Cause a textbook can't teach you everything. Now, a college degree may have been something that Thomas needed in his line of work, but what he do don't apply to you. I mean, you got a good job here – with plenty of opportunity to grow. Plus I figure, I'm gonna need somebody with good sense to run this place when I retire.

Kenny: *[Surprised]* You mean?

Joe: Well, I ain't got no children of my own to entrust it to. And I'd like to know that whenever I do decide to let it go somebody who has the wherewithal is running things. I wouldn't want my hard work to be in vain.

Kenny: *[Excited]* And it wouldn't be, Mr. Warren! I promise you I'd run this place like a fine tuned machine...

Joe: Now, don't you be getting your mind fixed on nothing. I'm far from retiring.

Kenny: I know, Mr. Warren. I'm just honored you'd consider me, that's all.

Joe: Well, I'm gonna be in the back room breaking them crates down. If it get too busy up here just holler, hear?

Kenny: Sure thing!

Joe exits to the back. The lights go down.

Scene Three

Later that Evening

The lights come up on the tavern. It's closing time. Joe is counting the money in the register. Kenny is behind the counter cleaning mugs. Leon is at the jukebox listening to his song.

Joe: *[Handing Kenny the money]* Here, double count this money for me.

Kenny: *[Proudly]* Yes, sir.

Joe: *[To Leon]* And don't you bother putting another nickel in that jukebox, cause that's the last tune for the evening. *[Leon waves Joe off. There's a knock at the door].* Whoever that is tell'em we're closed.

Leon: The owner say he closed! *[The knocking continues].* Nigga, didn't you hear me – he said he closed!

Joe walks over to the door. There's an old man standing outside the door.

Joe: I'm sorry, sir, but we're closed.

Reginald: *[Outside]* Alderman Phillips sent me here.

Joe opens the door.

Joe: What he send you here for?

Reginald: Shelter.

Joe: He told me that he wasn't sending ya'll here until tomorrow morning.

Reginald: He ain't tell me that. He just told me to go down to Joe's Tavern and ask for a fella by the name of Joseph Warren. He say he gonna give me a place to stay. Is Joseph Warren around?

Joe: Yeah, I'm Joseph Warren.

Reginald: Then you just the man I wanna see. *[Extending his hand]*. My name is Reginald O' Connor.

Joe: *[Reluctantly]* Nice to meet you, Mr. O' Connor.

Reginald: Please, call me Reginald. I mean, you giving me a place to sleep and all, the least I can do is let you call me by my first name. Know it don't sound like much, but its great meaning in my name. Do you know what Reginald means?

Joe: Nah.

Reginald: It means "King", and a king wouldn't allow nobody to call'em by his first name, so it's more of a privilege than you think. Now, as far as the other half of my name, well, that come from a long line of mixing and things...

Joe: Well, Mr. O' Connor...

Reginald: *[Insisting]* Reginald.

Joe: Reginald, I'm closing up things right now and I got somewhere to be in a little while, so could you come back in the morning?

Reginald: What sense would it make to come back in the morning when I'm standing here right now?

Joe: Look, Alderman Phillips told me that he wasn't sending ya'll here until tomorrow morning, and that's what I was expecting. So it be best if you just come back then.

Reginald: So what you telling me is I got to spend another night on the street because you wasn't expecting me until tomorrow morning?

Joe: That's right. It's warm outside – another night won't hurt you.

Reginald: What difference do that make? Warm air don't make the ground any more comfortable. *[Waving Joe off]* Ah, don't you worry about it though. I'm sorry I even bothered you. Maybe I shouldn't have come tonight. Guess I got excited when I heard I didn't have to spend another night on the street, but it's alright. I'll just make myself comfortable over there in the alley.

Reginald starts on his way.

Joe: *[Reluctantly]* Reginald. Come on in. I'll take you up as soon as I finish closing.

Reginald: You sure?

Joe: I'm sure. *[Reginald enters. Joe locks the door behind him].* You can have a seat over here until I finish.

Reginald: Good evening, fella's.

Kenny: Evening.

Reginald sits down at the bar counter. He looks around.

Reginald: Nice place you got here.

Joe: Thanks.

Reginald: How long have you had it?

Joe: For three years now.

Reginald: That's good. I like to see a black man running his own business. Show you that we've come a long way. I mean, we still got a ways to go, but at least we heading in the right direction, wouldn't you say?

Joe: Yes, sir, I'd say *some* of us are.

Reginald: Yes indeed.

Leon: So what's your angle? Can't find no work?

Reginald: Nah, I ain't had much luck finding nothing since I was let go from my last job.

Leon: And how long ago was that?

Reginald: Oh, I'd have to say about - ten years.

Leon: *[Condescending]* Ten years! Sounds more like you retired.

Joe: What kind'a work did you do?

Reginald: I was a United States Postman.

Joe: No kidding.

Reginald: Yeah, I delivered mail in this city for twenty years. It was the only job I really enjoyed. Then one morning the Post Master requested to see me in his office. He told me they had to let me go because I had served time in Mississippi twenty years before I moved up here.

Joe: Well, what you serve time for?

Reginald: A little skirmish.

Joe: I ain't never known nobody to serve time for a little skirmish.

Reginald: Well, I reckon you ain't never lived in Mississippi.

Leon: What living in Mississippi got to do with the law putting you behind bars?

Reginald: Because it's all about *who* you get into a fight with that determines your sentence. You see, the law don't work the same for *everybody* in the south, if you know what I mean.

Joe: Did you explain that to your Post Master?

Reginald: I sure did, but he said it wasn't nothing he could do. As far as Mississippi authorities were concerned I had broken the law, and the Post Office couldn't keep a convicted felon employed.

Joe: Well, that's the law – ain't no way around it.

Reginald: And that I couldn't argue with. But what bothered me most was later on I found out the Post Office knew about my criminal record all along. They were just waiting to fire me before I reached my pension date. Well, after learning that it took me a long time to get up enough confidence to look for other work. Cant' find many jobs that pay as well as the Postal Service. Some men got to work two or three jobs to match it. And I ain't never seen much sense in working two or three jobs - not to live one life.

Leon: *[Condescending]* Well, some of us do what's necessary to live comfortably.

Leon exits to the bathroom.

Reginald: Oh, I don't have anything against a man who works several jobs to live. It just wasn't gonna work out that way for me.

Joe: *[Condescending]* Well, evidently! You been out of work for ten years

Reginald: That flier out there say Muddy Waters supposed to be here tomorrow night. Is that true?

Joe: Sure is.

Reginald: *[Reminiscing]* Old Muddy Waters – wonder what he singing these days. You know, me and Muddy was good friends years ago.

Joe: Is that right?

Reginald: Yep. We grew up together in Issaquena County in Mississippi. We did everything together. Of course that was before everybody knew him as "Muddy Waters".

Joe: Oh, yeah? And how old was he when he started playing the guitar?

Reginald: He had to be about fifteen years old, I guess. But he played the harp long before he started playing the guitar. And he was pretty good at that too. Wasn't a better harp player than me though.

Joe: *[Skeptical]* You play the harmonica?

Reginald: Sure do. Been playing it since I was six years old. In fact, me, and Muddy start playing together at some of the parties and fish fries around town when we got to be a little older. But Muddy, he took it a whole lot more serious than I did. He was trying to make a name for himself, and he never looked back.

Joe: When's the last time ya'll seen each other?

Reginald: Oh, it's been many years ago. He probably wouldn't even recognize me if he saw me.

Joe: *[Sarcastically]* Yeah, I'm sure.

Pause

Reginald: What, you calling me a liar? *[Joe doesn't respond]* So you don't believe me, huh? You think because I live on the street I can't know nobody famous? I mean, just cause I know somebody that got some money don't mean it rub off on me. Hell, I know a man who sleep two alleys down from here that's related to Sonny Liston. Could be his brother the way they resemble. And I know an older lady who say she Billie Holidays auntie. Don't know if that's true or not, but she got photographs of her.

Joe: Look, Reginald, I ain't mean nothing by that. I just find it kind'a hard to believe.

Reginald: I don't know why. You don't know nothing about me except for what I've told you. That is, unless you gonna make a determination based on how I look. But you can't judge a man from his appearance until you know his story. But I bet you the kind'a fella who writes a man's story for him. *[He points to the scar on his face].* You see this scar on my face and assume I been involved in something mischievous – been up to no good, huh?. But little do you know it was a white man who done this to me. Now, you assume that I was attempting to steal from that white man for him to cut me across the face. But I ain't never stole nothing from nobody. Truth is, I was protecting my sister from being raped. But you probably don't believe that either, cause you so set on the fact that I live on the street. I must've done something to be living this way, yeah? Well, for your information, I could've sold thousands of records just like Muddy Waters if I had been given the chance. Could've been touring the world too. But it's hard to record an album when you're laid up in jail for ten years. And when you finally get the chance to show what you got the studios ain't interested in solo harp players no more. Now, you can choose to believe it or not, but that's my story – the hand that I was dealt. And it's plenty of other folks living on the street with stories like mine, but don't nobody give a damn cause we ain't got nothing to show for.

Joe: Now, I ain't said all that. All I said was I found it hard to believe that you and Muddy Waters were good friends. And maybe my reasons for thinking that way had something to do with you being homeless, but I ain't mean for you to be taking it beyond that. And if I offended you, I apologize. I don't think any less of homeless folks than I do of folks with homes. But I understand that there are some fools who are just plain lazy, and then there are men who have just been dealt a bad hand. But you can't think of one set of folks without considering the other. That's just the way it is.

Reginald: Well, I can't argue with that. Got folks that ain't no good on both ends. And I guess you wouldn't be offering shelter to some of us street rats if you were partial, so I too apologize.

Joe: Hey, ain't no big deal. Say, why don't we have a drink.

Reginald: Alright with me.

Joe pours some drinks. Leon enters from the bathroom.

Leon: Pour me one too why you at it.

Joe: Okay, but this is your last one. I gotta get out of here soon.

Leon sits down at the bar.

Leon: I don't know why you closing so early tonight. Wednesday nights one of your busiest, ain't it?

Joe: Yeah, but I got things to do tonight.

Leon: What you got to do that's more important than making money?

Joe: I got a date.

Leon: You closing the tavern early over a woman? Man, you must be losing your mind!

Joe: This ain't just any woman – it's a special woman.

Leon: Ain't no woman worth losing good money over.

Joe: Eunice Johnson is.

Leon: You a goddamn liar! You ain't got no date with Eunice Johnson.

Joe: Do too. I asked her out a few weeks ago, cause unlike you I schedule my dates in advance.

Leon: Not with Eunice Johnson you didn't.

Joe: I sure did. In fact, she wanted to go out sooner, but I told her I couldn't because I had business to tend to. But I promised her that if she were willing to wait a week, I'd close the tavern early tonight just to be with her. Man, that woman start to smiling like it wasn't no tomorrow, and last I checked she was still grinning from ear to ear.

Leon: Well, I don't give a damn *who* it is. Ain't *no* woman worth all that.

Joe: You see, that's why you ain't had a woman in years. You don't know how to treat'em. Got to show'em that you interested. Do things that make them wonder where you been all their lives. See, closing a few hours early ain't hurt me none, cause I figure I'll make it up tomorrow night. But to her it mean the world, cause she figure I'm willing to stop business just to be with her. It's the little things like that that make a woman feel good.

 Leon: Closing the tavern four hours early ain't no little thing. You could be losing good money tonight. Why don't you let Kenny close up for you?

Joe: Cause Kenny can't do it by himself.

Kenny: And Kenny got plans of his own tonight.

Leon: Well, what about me? I can close up for you. Just tell me what to do and I'll make sure everything is done right.

Joe: Nigga, is you mad! If I left you to close up I wouldn't have no liquor to sell tomorrow.

Joe and Kenny laugh.

Leon: Oh, I see now. You think I'm a drunk, huh?

Joe: Well, every day you the first one in here and the last one to leave. You spend every free hour you got in here drinking. You said it yourself, liquor is what keep you running. Can't go to work without it – can't go to sleep without it. Now, you tell me what I'm supposed to think.

Leon: *[Offended]* I may drink a lot, but I ain't no damn drunk.

Joe: Then one night away from the bar won't hurt you none. Besides, there ain't nothing you can do when the filling station is closed for the evening, but fill up the next morning. Hell, it might do you some good.

Leon: *[Slightly inebriated and perturbed]* Nigga, I don't need you to determine what's good for me. I can manage my goddamn self. Shit, you don't see me standing in that line across the street asking for no handouts. Nor am I sleeping in the alley like this nigga here. I got me a steady job with a nice home and a fine automobile that sit in front of it.

Joe: And that may be true. Like I told you earlier, I don't give a damn how much you drink when you come up in here as long as you got the means to cover it. I'm just trying to protect my investment. You see, nigga's who overdo it tend to get destructive with things around here. Just last week I found myself re-hinging a door, and wiping piss from the walls.

Leon: So what you telling me for? I ain't the one responsible for that.

Joe: And I'm just taking precaution to make sure it ain't you. That's why I'm cutting you off now, while I know you still got enough sense to open a door properly and piss directly in the stall.

Leon: Don't you be putting limits on my drinking cause some other fool can't hold his liquor.

Joe: Like I said, I'm just protecting my business.

Leon: That's fine, but don't cut me off over what some other nigga done. Hell, if I wanna drink myself to *death* that ain't no business of yours.

Joe: Nah, it ain't, but it's plenty of business *for* me. Shit, I ain't got enough liquor in this tavern to satisfy you let alone kill you. So if you wanna drink yourself to death, be my guest. Just make sure that money is sitting on the counter before you drop dead.

Reginald: Now what's all this talk about death? You're still a young man with plenty of life left in you. I mean, you ain't getting no younger, but you still ain't old enough to be establishing no will.

Joe: That's right. You ought'a listen to the man, Leon. Hell, you may even find you a nice gal and decide to settle down again someday. And you gonna wanna hold on to your family that time around.

Leon: *[Angry]* What the hell you trying to say! I didn't do a good job of holding on to my family?!

Joe: You tell me. They ain't here now, are they?

Leon slings an empty glass at Joe. The glass misses him and hits the back wall.

Leon: *[Explosive]* You keep my family out your goddamn mouth!

Joe grabs his bat from behind the bar counter and rushes Leon.

Joe: *[Angry]* You want a piece of me?! Come get some then!

Kenny jumps between the two men.

Kenny: It ain't worth it, Mr. Warren. That's just drunk talk coming out of him.

Joe: Get the hell out'a here for I put this bat across your head.

Kenny: *[To Leon]* You need to go on home now, Leon.

Leon reaches in his pocket and pulls out some money. He places the money on the bar counter and exits.

Joe: And don't you ever bring your drunk ass back in here! You ain't welcome here no more, you hear – no more!

Reginald: That fella got something awful on him.

Joe: Yeah, the devil!

Reginald: Well, if you know the devil like I know him, you know it won't be the last you see of him.

Black out.

ACT TWO

Scene One

The Next Morning

The lights come up on the tavern. Kenny is cleaning the bar counter. Moments later, Rashied enters.

Rashied: Good morning, brotha!

Kenny: Hey Rashied, what's going on?

Rashied: I just came by to let you know I spoke with the Minister Malcolm briefly last night after our meeting. I mentioned you and your desire to hear him speak in person. So he said that if you attended our service this Sunday he'd be more than happy to talk to you afterward.

Kenny: *[Excited]* You kidding!

Rashied: Nah, brotha, those were his exact words. In fact, he's looking forward to meeting you.

Kenny: What did you tell him about me?

Rashied: I just told him that you were an ambitious young man who was hungry for the truth.

Kenny: Well, I appreciate that, and I'll most definitely be there. *[Discretely]* I can't let Mr. Warren know that though. He'd be sore with me if he ever found out.

Rashied: No worries. It's just between us.

Kenny continues to clean the bar counter.

Kenny: After you left yesterday I started thinking about that Lynch fella you were talking about.

Rashied: Yeah? What about him?

Kenny: You know – his teachings and things. I can't help but believe that some of what you were saying is true.

Rashied: Correction, brotha – *all* of it is true. I mean, look at the condition of our people today. Have you ever seen such division amongst mankind. You can't find a more disenfranchised culture of people on the entire earth. And who's doctrine could create such a device to hold an entire race of people mentally captive, but the devil himself.

Kenny: What do you mean when you say device?

Rashied: I mean it's a tool that works to preserve the conditioning of this wicked doctrine. And these devices could be anything from drugs, *alcohol*, even education. *[Kenny exhibits befuddlement].* Oh, don't look surprised, brotha. Since the very first day you stepped foot inside of a school you were being taught from fraudulent material. That's right! We've been fed lies since birth, all administered by the Board of Education. I tell you there is nothing in this world more legitimate than this here. *[He lifts his Koran].* Allah is the only way to the truth.

Mr. Rainey enters.

Kenny: Good morning, Mr. Rainey.

Rainey: Morning, Kenny – Rashied.

Rashied: Good morning.

Rainey sits down at the bar. Kenny pours him a cup of coffee.

Rainey: Where's Joseph?

Kenny: Upstairs helping some folks get settled in.

Rainey: Thomas' people done finally moved in, huh?

Kenny: Nah, these are homeless folks.

Rainey: Homeless? What he getting them settled in for? They can't pay rent.

Kenny: The rent already been paid. I'm sure Mr. Warren will tell you all about it.

Joe enters. He shows disgust as he looks at Rashied.

Joe: Now, if any of them other fella's from the Nation were to see you coming around this place like you do, they'd start to wonder if you in here doing the bidding of Allah or the devil.

Rashied: Allah knows my purpose for being in here, and that's all that matters.

Joe: Well, if your bible read anything like mine do, there's a passage in it that says: "Don't let your good be evil spoken of". Your purpose may be pure as gold, but even gold starts to melt the more time it spends in the incinerator. I mean, listen to all the rumors surrounding your *great* leader. Folks is saying that he done fathered two or three children outside his marriage. Don't know whether it's true or not, but that's what folks are saying.

Rashied: You must be careful, brotha. Propaganda is the devils rhetoric, and it spews out of mouths like venom from a serpent. You can't believe nothing you read from the white man's paper. It's their job to disparage our leaders and cause division amongst are people.

Joe: You ever thought that maybe it was one of your people who gave the white man that information? I mean, who else would know something so private?

Rashied: No matter the source, I assure you, nothing could be further from the truth.

Joe: Well, I guess only time will tell, huh?

Rashied: Yes, brotha, time will indeed reveal all things. *[Rashied rises* *from his bar stool].* Well, I better be on my way. I'll talk to you brotha's later.

Kenny: See you around, Rashied.

Rashied exits the tavern.

Joe: You see there. He know I ain't lying. And I bet what the newspapers are saying about Muhammad is all true. Hell, he ain't no different than any other man. If a nigga got an itch, he gonna scratch it.

Rainey: That's sho' nough the truth.

Joe: I'm surprised to see you in here so early, Mr. Rainey. I wasn't expecting you until this evening.

Rainey: I didn't have nothing else to do this morning, so I figured I'd come down here and get me a hot cup of coffee and a good conversation. That's always a good way to start off the day. You know, when you get to live as old as me, a hot cup of coffee and a good conversation hold a lot of weight.

Joe: Well, you know you'll always find that in here.

Rainey: And I certainly appreciate it.

Joe: What about Lorraine? What she do with her time when ya'll apart?

Rainey: Oh, she may be straightening up around the place, or reading an article she might have found interesting in today's paper. That's what she normally do while I'm gone. But I don't leave her alone at home too often. I just step away long enough to give her a little time to herself. I wouldn't want her to grow tired of me.

Joe: Well, I bet you appreciate the little time you spend away from home too.

Rainey: Yeah, it's nice. But I enjoy Lorraine's company, so I don't like to stay gone for too long.

Joe: And how long ya'll been married?

Rainey: Forty two years.

Joe: Ain't that something? Forty two years of marriage and you still can't get enough of your old lady. That's a beautiful thing.

Rainey: Well, Lorraine ain't never been the kind'a woman that make a man dread being at home. If I didn't think I bothered her so much I'd never leave the house.

Kenny: That sound a lot different from some of the stories I've heard, especially from the men that come in here; talking bout how their old ladies always fussing and carrying on. It kind'a make me wonder what's the good in being married.

Rainey: Oh, it's plenty good in being married. The trick is marrying the right woman - the woman that fit you best.

Kenny: But how you supposed to know who the right woman is? Ain't no woman gonna show too much of her ugliness before you marry her.

Rainey: Sure they do. It just don't always appear to be ugly, but the signs are always there. You just got to know how to read'em.

Joe: I sure wish I had known how to read'em before I married Vickie. That woman ran circles around me.

Rainey: So I take it you and Bernadette wanna be married, huh?

Kenny: Someday, but that ain't soon enough for her.

Rainey: Well, Bernadette is a nice girl, and she come from a respectable family. Her father's a minister – mothers a missionary. You know she got to do it the right way. Can't just be out here casually. She got to be spoken for, and that's a good thing. Shows she ain't no loose woman.

Kenny: Nah, not at all. It's only so far she let me go before she push me off of her.

Rainey: See there, that's a good one. Can't see her giving you no problems in marriage.

Joe: Kenny, get on back there and pack them beer cases.

Kenny: Yes, sir.

Kenny exits back.

Joe: Please don't talk about marriage with that boy, Mr. Rainey. He way too young to be thinking about them kind'a things.

Rainey: He twenty one years old, ain't he? Three years older than you were when you got married.

Joe: Yeah, but I had better sense at eighteen than he do.

Rainey: I don't know about that. He got enough sense to marry him a girl that's gonna do right by him. Can't say the same for you. You married a scoundrel.

Joe: If only that offended me.

They laugh.

Rainey: What's this I hear about you helping some folks get settled in upstairs?

Joe: I agreed to help Alderman Phillips get some folks off the streets for a little while.

Rainey: That was nice of you.

Joe: Well, you know I ain't the charitable type, but the alderman covered their rent. It took him twelve hundred dollars to sway me though.

Rainey: That's a lot of money.

Joe: Sure is, but he insisted.

Rainey: What about them other folks who were supposed to be moving in here?

Joe: They're still moving in. It'll just be a month later than we had planned. But it worked out well cause now I can use the money the alderman paid me to fix up the place.

Rainey: That's good thinking.

Reginald enters.

Joe: There's one of the fella's now. Morning, Reginald.

Reginald: Good morning.

Joe: How'd you sleep last night?

Reginald: Some of the best sleep I got in years.

Joe: Hey, this is my good friend Floyd Rainey. Mr. Rainey, this is Reginald O' Connor.

Reginald: Nice to meet you.

Rainey: Same here.

Reginald sits down at the bar.

Joe: Can I get you something this morning, Reginald?

Reginald: A cup of coffee be nice.

Joe: Coming right up.

Reginald: You seen that line outside the office across the street? You can't even see where it end it's so long.

Rainey: It's been like that for a while now.

Reginald: Didn't know it was that many folks living in this community, let alone out of work.

Joe sets a cup of coffee in front of Reginald.

Joe: Alderman Phillips said it wasn't much he could do about it other than advise the people to go elsewhere to take care of their business.

Rainey: Make you wonder what the other offices in the city look like. Probably just as bad.

Reginald: So how was your date last night?

Joe: Man, it was wonderful! We had us a really good time.

Rainey: You been holding out on me, Joseph? Who you seeing now?

Joe: If I told you you wouldn't believe me.

Rainey: Try me.

Joe: Eunice Johnson.

Rainey: I don't believe it.

Joe: See, what I tell you. Everybody I done told say the same thing. I don't know why it's so hard to believe. Ain't nothing wrong with me. I'm entitled to the best, ain't I?

Rainey: Of course you are. It's just that you ain't never mentioned her, that's all. I think ya'll make a fine couple.

Reginald: This Eunice Johnson must be a sight to behold.

Rainey: Most beautiful young woman in all Chicago if you ask me. And she's a real sweet girl too. You'd better lock that down, Joseph.

Joe: I'm just taking it slow. My last marriage took a lot out of me. I ain't trying to rush into nothing like that again.

Rainey: Eunice and Vickie are like night and day. You can't be comparing the two.

Joe: I ain't. I just wanna make sure everything is right first.

Reginald: Well, don't take too long, especially if she the kind'a woman you say she is. Take too long and some other fella gonna come around and snatch her from right under your nose.

Rainey: That's right.

Joe: I won't.

Rainey: Well, I guess I'll be on my way.

Joe: Alright. I'll see you this evening.

Rainey: I'll see ya'll.

Rainey exits.

Reginald: Nice fella.

Joe: Yeah, he's good people.

Reginald: Seems to be.

Joe: Say, you ever been married?

Reginald: Yeah, I was married for twenty years.

Joe: Good years?

Reginald: Great years!

Joe: What happened?

Reginald: She died nearly ten years ago.

Joe: I'm sorry to hear that.

Reginald: Ain't nothing to be sorry for. That woman was too good for this world. Wasn't no better place fit for her but heaven.

Joe: That's some kind'a woman.

Reginald: She was some kind'a wonderful, I tell you – a great woman to know.

Joe: Got any children?

Reginald: Nah, Sarah couldn't have none. Doctors say she was barren… caused by an illness of some sort. It didn't make me no difference though. She was all I ever needed. She was my everything, and when I lost her I lost everything. I lost my whole purpose of living. Only thing I live for now is seeing her again.

Joe: That's nice. I reckon you ain't trying to see her no time too soon though.

Reginald: Too soon ain't soon enough for me, not when it come to seeing my Sarah again. Them other folks get here yet?

Joe: Early this morning.

Reginald: How many?

Joe: Just five of'em.

Reginald: Well, I guess I'd better go introduce myself since we gonna be neighbors and all. I may even know a few of'em.

Reginald rises from the bar counter.

Joe: Hey, Reginald, what exactly did the alderman tell you about coming here?

Reginald: Well, just like I told you last night: He say a man by the name of Joseph Warren was offering shelter in his apartment building. Gave me the name of the building and the address and told me to come on down. He said everything was taken care of.

Joe: Did he tell you that it was only temporary?

Reginald: Nah, he ain't mention that. But I figured it would be. Ain't nothing ever permanent.

Joe: Estella should be sending your breakfast soon. When it comes would you serve everybody?

Reginald: Sure thing.

As Reginald starts to the door Thomas enters. They stare at each other in crossing. Reginald exits.

Thomas: Whose that?

Joe: That's Reginald. He's one of the people the alderman sent down here.

Thomas: Figures.

Joe: Here. *[Joe hands Thomas a large envelope].* They're all signed and dated.

Thomas: I called the *real* tenants and told them that they would have to wait an extra month before moving in.

Joe: Oh yeah? What they say?

Thomas: They weren't happy about the setback, but they still intend to move in.

Joe: Then that's all that matters.

Thomas: Now, Joseph, you're going to have to make sure those people are gone in two months, or else we're going to lose a lot of money.

Joe: I told you, they only gonna be here for two months. Ain't no need to worry about that.

Thomas: I hope not. Hey, fix me a cup of coffee.

Joe pours Thomas a cup of coffee. Kenny enters.

Kenny: *[To Thomas]* Hey, Mr. Fleming.

Thomas: Hey! I brought you something.

Thomas removes a catalog from his brief case and hands it to Kenny.

Kenny: What's this?

Thomas: It's a college catalog. Every school in this state is listed in there.

Kenny: *[Indifferent]* Thanks, Mr. Fleming.

Thomas: You give any thought to what we talked about yesterday?

Kenny: I thought about it some. Still ain't certain if it's for me though.

Thomas: Sure it is, it's for everybody. Keep in mind, college is a higher form of education, and everyone is entitled to it. Don't let the sound of it intimidate you.

Kenny: I'm just not sure whether I need it for my line of work, that's all.

Thomas: Well, what is it that you want to do?

Kenny: I suppose I'd like to own my own barbershop someday.

Thomas: Then college would definitely benefit you. As a business owner you're going to need great math and reading skills. Not to mention a vast knowledge of consumer economics.

Joe: Thomas, if the boy ain't too keen on going to college, who is you to convince him that he should. He a grown man – he know what he wanna do with his life.

Thomas: It's only advice. He don't have to adhere to it if he doesn't want to. I'm only looking out for his best interest. Let me ask you something, Kenny, what were your grades like in high school?

Kenny: Uh, I did alright, I guess.

Thomas: Well, I tell you what, go to your old high school in the morning and ask for your records, then we'll go from there.

Kenny: I'll try.

Thomas: Good. I'll see you later, Joe.

Thomas exits.

Joe: There ain't nothing they can teach you there that you can't learn on the job here.

Kenny: I know.

Joe: Well, look, I'm gonna run to the market down the street. Think you can handle it until I get back?

Kenny: Sure.

Joe: I got to make sure there's plenty of food for the crowd tonight, because it's gonna be a big one. *[Joe grabs his hat and starts to the door].* I'll be back.

Kenny: Alright.

Joe exits. Kenny picks up the phone and dials.

Kenny: *[On the phone]* Hey, how you doing, Mrs. Pointer? Is Bernadette around? Yes, ma'am. I'll keep it short. *[pause]* Hey, sweet thing! What you doing? I was thinking about you too. Naw, I got to work tonight. What about tomorrow? I get off early tomorrow. Can't you wait for all that? Ain't nothing wrong with your hair, girl. It always look the same to me. *[Leon enters the tavern. Kenny looks over at him].* Hey, I'ma have to call you back later.

Leon: Where's Joe?

Kenny: He ain't here.

Leon sits down at the bar counter.

Leon: Get me a Jack no ice.

Kenny: Mr. Warren told me not to serve you. He say you ain't welcome here no more.

Leon: I don't see him nowhere around here.

Kenny: Don't matter if he here or not. This is his place, and if he tell me not to serve you I ain't supposed to serve you.

Leon grabs Kenny by his collar.

Leon: Look, boy, you'd better make my drink before I come back there and make it myself.

Kenny: You'd better let me go if you know what's best for you.

Reginald enters.

Reginald: Now, from where I'm standing it look like you in here starting trouble.

Leon: This ain't no business of yours, old man.

Reginald: Nah, it ain't. But that boy got to be about two times younger than you, and he pretty solid for his age too. Years ago I tried to tussle with a young man that was about that boy age and he put a good hurting on me. Broke my arm and my hip, and they ain't been right ever since. So you may wanna let that boy go for he do the same to you.

Leon lets Kenny loose.

Leon: You tell Joseph I'm looking for him.

Kenny: You come tell him yourself. He'll be back in a few hours.

Leon exits. Reginald sits down at the bar.

Reginald: You alright, son?

Kenny: I'm alright.

Reginald: *[Playfully]* I just didn't want you to hurt him too bad.

Kenny: Can I get you something to drink?

Reginald: Got any orange juice? It's too early for anything else. *[Kenny pours him a glass of orange juice].* That fella can't get enough of this place, huh?

Kenny: It was like his second home.

Reginald: There's something wrong with a man who finds refuge in a tavern.

Kenny: That's what I've been telling Mr. Warren, but it's all the same to him. Leon ain't no different from nobody else, let Mr. Warren tell it.

Reginald: Well, that may be. But I ain't never known a man to surrender his refuge so easily.

Joe enters with an arm full of paper bags.

Joe: Hey, Kenny, give me a hand, would you?

Kenny: Yes, sir.

Kenny takes the bag from Joe and exits to the back.

Reginald: What you got there, Joe?

Joe: I went out and bought some food for tonight. *[Calling]* Kenny, put this grease on the counter for me.

Kenny: Sure thing.

Joe: I got more than two hundred chicken wings that need to be fried.

Reginald: That's a lot of chicken.

Joe: Well, I'm expecting a lot of folks tonight. Got to take advantage of every opportunity to make some extra money.

Reginald: I know what you mean. Just let me know if you need any help back there this evening.

Joe: Oh, I will. *[Kenny enters]* You put that grease on the counter like I told you?

Kenny: Yes, sir. And Leon came by looking for you.

Joe: What he want?

Kenny: He wanted a drink.

Joe: You didn't serve him, did you?

Kenny: No, sir - I told him to leave.

Joe: He give you a hard time?

Kenny: A little bit.

Joe: Did he tell you where he was going?

Kenny: Nah, but I'm sure he'll be back.

Joe: And when he does I got something for him.

Reginald: Now, ain't no sense in getting in trouble over no troubled man. Trouble'll find him on its own.

Joe: My patience done worn too thin with that fool. I can't have him coming in here and disturbing my business. He come back in here and it's gonna be me and him, and that's all to it. *[Joe exits to the back]* Kenny, make sure every keg is full out there. We got a long night ahead of us.

Kenny: Yes, sir.

The lights go down.

Scene Two

Next Morning

The lights come up on the tavern. Kenny is cleaning the mugs. Mr. Rainey is sitting at the bar drinking a cup of coffee.

Rainey: *[Singing]* All you little girls - standing out in that line – I can make love to you woman - in five minutes time - now ain't that a man?

Kenny: *[Yelling]* Sho' nough is!

Kenny slaps the bar counter. Joe enters from the back.

Joe: Boy, what the hell is wrong with you!

Kenny: I'm sorry, Mr. Warren.

Joe: Go out there and wipe them tables down, and act like you got some sense.

Kenny: Yes, sir.

Rainey: We were just singing one of Muddy's songs.

Joe: You enjoy yourself last night, Mr. Rainey?

Rainey: I sure did. It's about the second or third time I seen him play, but last night had to be one of the best.

Joe: Well, I'm glad you enjoyed it.

Rainey: And I enjoyed that fella up stairs too. He know he can play that harp.

Joe: Can't he though!

Rainey: Looked like him and Muddy known each other for years.

Joe: They grew up together in Mississippi.

Rainey: *[Surprised]* Is that right?

Joe: Uh huh. They go way back. Reginald told me that they used to play together when they were younger, but he just wasn't as serious about it as Muddy.

Rainey: Well, they sho' sounded good together.

Joe: Yeah, it's a shame that Reginald couldn't make no career out of it like Muddy did. Guess it ain't meant for everybody to prosper that way.

Rainey: It ain't never too late though. Ain't like you got to be a young man to play the Blues. He can still make a name for himself at his age. All he got to do is play and the folks will come. He can do well for himself given the opportunity he had last night.

Joe: Maybe so.

Rainey: And it be nice to have a musician here every once and a while. It's something to think about.

Joe: Kenny, where you put that bottle opener?

Kenny: I left it in the back.

Joe: What good is it gonna do us back there? We serve the liquor up here.

Kenny: Sorry, Mr. Warren.

Joe: You better start thinking, boy!

Joe exits to the back.

Rainey: Seems like Joseph ain't in the best of moods this morning.

Kenny: Mr. Warren? Aw, he like that every morning. Plus I got here later than usual. He say it throw him all off schedule when I get here late.

Rainey: Well, it was a long night. I could imagine you over sleeping a little.

Kenny: Oh, I didn't oversleep. I just had to make a quick stop at my old high school before I came here. I picked up my grades.

Rainey: What for? You been out of high school for over three years.

Kenny: Thomas Fleming told me to get my grades so he could take a look at'em. He trying to convince me to go to college. *[Kenny pulls his grades from his back pocket and places them in front of Mr. Rainey].* Here they go. Pretty decent, you think?

Rainey: Is that what all these D's stand for – decent?

Kenny snatches his grades and puts them back in his pocket.

Kenny: Wasn't my idea! I told him I wasn't the best student in high school, but he kept insisting.

Rainey: Well, maybe he know something that you don't.

Thomas enters.

Kenny: Hey there, Mr. Fleming.

ACT TWO

Thomas: Where's Joseph?

Kenny: He in the back. Hey, I went and got my grades this morning…

Thomas: I can't right now, Kenny. *[Yelling]* Joseph! Get out here!

Joe enters.

Joe: What's the problem?

Thomas: The agreement you made with the alderman is the problem. That check he wrote you - it wasn't any good.

Joe: What you mean it wasn't no good?

Thomas: Just like I said, the check bounced. The money wasn't available. It probably wasn't even a legitimate account.

Joe: Nah, that can't be. The alderman wouldn't write me no bad check. I know him better than that.

Thomas: Well, you obviously don't know him well enough, because you were deceived. I told you it was a bad idea from the beginning, but "he's a good man", you say. "He's just trying to take care of the community", you say. It's your place to help him, you say. But none of that means a damn thing now because you're providing shelter for six bum's who can't pay the rent.

Joe: It was a two month agreement. Why would the alderman write me a bad check knowing that I'd find out it wasn't no good in a few days time? That don't make no sense. I'm sure he got an explanation.

Thomas: There's no time to be seeking explanations, Joseph! Just accept it – you've been conned. Only thing to do now is put them out of here! That way you don't lose anything. And I'll call the other tenants I have lined up and tell them that they can move in as they originally scheduled.

Joe: You gonna have to wait on that, Thomas.

Thomas: What are we waiting for? If you put those people back on the street now we can move the other tenants in as soon as possible.

Joe: Kenny, I need you to watch the place for a little while. I got to make a run.

Kenny: Sure thing, Mr. Warren.

Joe grabs his hat.

Thomas: And where the hell are you going?

Joe: I'm going to see the alderman – try to find out what's happened.

Thomas: Well, then I'm coming with you. I don't need him talking you into anymore of his foolish schemes.

Joe and Thomas exit.

Kenny: Ain't that something? The alderman done wrote Mr. Warren a bad check. A 'big' bad check too.

Rainey: That's politics for you. They promise you a back rub and next thing you know you're bent over with your pants around your ankles, wondering how the hell you got in a position like that. But it ain't like Alderman Phillips to do nobody that way. He been a straight forward man since he been on the council; got to be something more to it. Like Joseph said, they had a two month agreement. Anybody know it only take two or three days to find out a check ain't no good.

Kenny: What you think happened then?

Rainey: I couldn't tell you. Could be a bank error for all we know. But I'm sure it ain't nothing like what Thomas speculating.

Kenny: All I know is he sure is trying to get them other tenants in here. They must be some really important people.

Rainey: Only thing important about them people he know is that they ain't from around here. Let Thomas tell it, there ain't a set of descent black folks for miles away. *[drinking the last of his coffee]* I'm gonna go on now, but I'll be back soon to find out what happened.

Kenny: Sure thing. I'll see you later.

Rainey exits. Kenny opens his college catalog and begins to look through it. Reginald enters.

Reginald: Hey there, young man.

Kenny: Hey, Reginald. Can I get you a drink?

Reginald: A cranberry juice be nice – not too much ice though.

Kenny makes the drink and places it in front of him.

Kenny: You sure was something last night. Where you learn how to play the harmonica like that?

Reginald: My Uncle Cletus. He taught me when I was just a little boy.

Kenny: And you and Muddy Waters grew up together, right?

Reginald: That's right. We were the best of friends.

Kenny: How long had it been since you last seen'em?

Reginald: A little over twenty five years ago.

Kenny: That's a long time.

Reginald: Well, we went in two different directions, you see? He chose music, and I – well, I ain't have much of a choice at all. I had to work like every other man, but ain't nothing wrong with that. It's just that you'd rather do something you gonna enjoy doing - know what I mean?

Kenny: Sure. If I didn't like it here I couldn't work the long hours I do.

Reginald: Well, you got to do what's necessary for the time being.

Kenny: Do it ever bother you that you ain't famous like Muddy?

Pause

Reginald: I believe it did at the beginning. But I was happy for him nonetheless. He worked hard for it. Wasn't no sense in being mad over it.

Kenny: I know it would have bothered me.

Reginald: Well, I found peace in knowing that I was just as good. Things just didn't unfold for me like they did Muddy. And there may not be nobody who'll come along and sing the Blues quite like him, but ain't nobody *lived* them quite as well as me, and that I take pride in.

Kenny: Why's that?

Reginald: Because it take a lot for a battered man to rise above his circumstances. And it took me a long time to recognize that. But when I did, I found the strength to carry on without any regrets.

Kenny: I reckon it take an awfully strong minded person to do that.

Reginald: Well, I don't know whether it was due to me having a strong mind, or the fact that life would rather have me carry it out, cause death sure didn't show no interest in me – even when I desired it most. And boy, there was some times when I really cried out for him. But this here harp became more than just an instrument to me. It became my companion in moments of trouble, and it got me through some of the roughest times.

Kenny: I bet it did. *[Alderman Phillips enters].* Alderman Phillips.

Reginald: Hey there, Alderman.

Phillips: Hey, Reginald. *[To Kenny]* Is Joseph here?

Kenny: Nah, he out looking for you. He left here about an hour ago.

Phillips: Damn!

Phillips sits down at the bar in a depressed manner.

Reginald: You alright, Alderman?

Phillips: Far from it.

Reginald: I sure wanna thank you for helping a few of us get off the streets for a little while. This a nice place here, and Joseph Warren is a real nice fella. He see to it that we get everything we need.

Phillips: You may not wanna be thanking me just yet. *[To Kenny]* Could you pour me a Bourbon?

Kenny: Sure.

Kenny makes the drink. Joe enters.

Joe: There you are. I've been looking all over for you.

Alderman Phillips stands to his feet.

Phillips: Joseph, I know you're angry, but I can explain.

Joe: What's the big idea, you writing me a bad check?

Phillips: It wasn't a bad check.

Joe: That ain't what the bank said. They said the money wasn't available.

Phillips: Listen, the reason the money wasn't available is because the city council put a hold on the account.

Joe: A hold? What for?

Phillips: Apparently they don't like the way I'm using the money. They think I ought'a be spending it on far more important things than housing the homeless.

Joe: Can they really do that?

Phillips: The mayor and his council can do whatever they want. They're the ones who disperse the annual budget to each Ward in the city.

Joe: But you're an alderman. Don't that count for anything? Ain't you got any say in the matter?

Phillips: Yeah, but it would count for even more if I were the alderman of a less poverty stricken community. Unfortunately, they only allow me so much authority when it comes to things like this. You know how it is.

Joe: *[Disappointed]* Yeah, I know.

Phillips: Look, I realize we had an agreement, but I'm not gonna be able to follow through with it. So of course you're not obligated to either. I'm really sorry, Joseph.

Joe: It ain't your fault. Your hands been tied and there ain't nothing you can do.

Brief silence.

Phillips: *[To Reginald]* Reginald, would you tell the others to come down. You can't stay here any longer.

Reginald: I'll go get'em.

Reginald starts to the door.

Joe: Wait, Reginald. *[To Phillips]* If I let'em stay would Estella still provide the meals?

Phillips: I don't know, but I'm sure we can work something out. Both of you mentioned that you needed some work done in your buildings. Maybe I can get a contractor out here to take a look at'em. I can't promise you anything, but I don't think the council would have any problem with that, seeing as it's *their* contractors. I'll put a request in on Monday morning. I'll give you a call as soon as I know something. Would that be alright?

Joe: Alright.

Phillips: I'll talk to you next week then.

Alderman Phillips exits.

Reginald: That was a really nice thing you done there, Joseph.

Kenny: It sure was, Mr. Warren.

Joe: Well, I figure I ain't really losing too much money as long as you covering everybody's rent.

Reginald: Covering they rent? How you expecting I do that? You know I ain't got no money, or no job for that matter.

Joe: You do now. That is if you wanna come work for me.

Reginald: What kind'a work you got in mind? I can't do no heavy lifting.

Joe: All I want you to do is play your harmonica three nights a week, and you and the others can stay here as long as you need. What do you say?

Reginald: *[Excited]* When do you want me to start?

Joe and Reginald shake hands.

Joe: Good.

Thomas enters.

Thomas: Was that the alderman I saw leaving from here?

Joe: Sure was.

Thomas: And what did he have to say for himself?

Joe: Not much.

Thomas: That figures. Snakes don't talk.

Joe: Come to find out the city council put a hold on the account. They didn't want him spending the money on shelter for the homeless.

Thomas: And I can't blame them. The city's money shouldn't be used to harbor the homeless. If anything, these people should be trying to find honest work instead of begging for everyone else's hard earned money. You can't help those who don't want to help themselves. And the alderman should know better than that. He can't abuse his position that way. He'll lose it the next time around.

Joe: Well, he'll always have my vote.

Thomas: I declare, if you haven't learned a lesson from what just happened you will later on. So are you going to put those people out, or would you prefer I did it?

Joe: We ain't putting nobody out, Thomas. I decided to let them stay for as long as they need to.

Thomas tries to keep his composure.

Thomas: Joseph, you'd better think long and hard about what you're doing. Now I know you want to help everyone and all, but you're a business man. And those bums you got living up stairs can't pay the rent. And if your rent isn't paid the mortgage won't be paid. You can't afford to give anything away for free. Your business won't prosper that way. That's why I'm here; to make sure you make wise business decisions. And this here is not a wise decision. I can't let you do this.

Joe: Look, Thomas, I know you looking out for my best interest, and I appreciate it. You've done a fine job. But it's my business, and I've already made up my mind. I'm letting them stay – every one of'em. Now, I still got four other rooms available if you still wanna move those other tenants in here.

Thomas: They're not going to go for that. And why should they? It wasn't part of our proposal. I promised each of them a safe and secure living environment, not a bum infested shelter.

Joe: Well, then maybe you ought'a find them something in the suburbs where they ain't got to live amongst the bums.

Brief silence.

Thomas: Alright. I see you've made up your mind, and a small mind it is. I can't help you anymore, Joseph – not if you can't adhere to my advice. I can't stand along side as your consultant and watch you destroy your business this way. *[Thomas places the documents on the bar counter].* So long, Joseph.

Joe: *[Solemnly]* So long.

Thomas exits.

Kenny: What you gonna do now, Mr. Warren?

Joe: There's only one thing I can do. I'm gonna sit down here and read through this stuff carefully till I figure out what it all mean. I can always call the IRS if I don't understand something. Hell, they wanna make sure they get everything that's due to them anyway. They'll be happy to hear from me.

Joe exits to the back. Moments later, Mr. Rainey enters.

Kenny: Hey, Mr. Rainey.

Rainey: Hey – Reginald!

Reginald: Hey!

Rainey: They make it back yet?

Kenny: Yeah. Mr. Warren in the back.

Rainey: Did he tell you what happened?

Kenny: Turned out that the city put a hold on the account. Wasn't no wrong doing by the Alderman.

Rainey: I figured that much. *[To Rainey]* So when am I gonna get a chance to hear you play that harp again?

Reginald: Sooner than I'd ever thought. Joe –

A distraught looking Leon enters the tavern.

Rainey: Oh, hey there, Leon. Where you been? I ain't seen you around in a few days.

Leon doesn't respond.

Kenny: *[Calling out]* Mr. Warren!

Joe enters from the back.

Joe: What is it, boy? *[Joe looks over at Leon. He grabs his bat from under the counter]* What the hell you want?! Didn't I tell you not to come up in here no more!

Leon: If I still had my damn job I wouldn't be here right now, but thanks to you I ain't got it no more.

Joe: What you mean, thanks to me? I ain't the one to be thanking. You can thank yourself for that.

Leon: Wasn't no right of yours to tell my boss I been drinking everyday before work.

Joe: Fool, I ain't told your boss no such thing! Where you think I find the time to be calling your boss?! I don't give a damn what you do on your job!

Leon: Then why all a sudden my boss fire me on suspicion that I be drinking on the job? Ain't nobody said nothing to me before.

Joe: Cause don't nobody care until you start to messing up things! Folks is fed up with you, Leon! You can't be blaming everybody else for your problems. Time you start taking responsibility for your own actions.

Leon: *[Explosive]* Don't you talk to me like you better than me!

Leon draws a gun on Joe.

Rainey: Leon, put that gun away!

Reginald: You pull that trigger and you gonna be in a hell'a trouble, boy. You don't wanna ruin your life that way.

Leon: He done ruined my life already!

Joe: You pull a gun on a man you best be ready to use it.

Rainey: Ain't no use for all that. You need to sit down and talk about this like men!

Leon: Damn all that! We're beyond talking.

Joe: Ain't like he ever listened anyway. If he had he wouldn't be standing here right now without a job.

Rainey: Joseph, you ain't making it no better now!

Joe: I don't give a damn! Ain't no making it better with him. He a lost cause. It's always the same thing with him. He go out there, cut up, then when trouble comes he blame everybody but himself. He know it's true. *[To Leon]* So what you gonna do, Leon? You gonna pull that trigger or not? Make a decision, fool! You seem sober enough.

Reginald: Don't you allow a man to tell your story for you. Tell it yourself! Tell him the real reason you come in here to shoot him dead.

Leon: What!

Reginald: Let him tell it, you just a drunk who can't accept responsibility for his own actions. But I know it's more to it than that.

Leon: You don't know me, old man!

Reginald: Boy, I know you better than you think. I figured you out the minute I laid eyes on you. We're similar - you and me. We both carrying around a whole lot of pain - pain that the average man can't bear. Only difference is we don't conceal it the same way.

Leon: What the hell you talking about!

Reginald: Your story is what I'm talking about! Can't no man tell your story like you can. Tell him what it is that draw you to this tavern. Tell him what it is! *[Leon doesn't respond]*. It ain't the liquor at all, is it?

There's a brief silence.

Leon: *[Saddened]* It's peace – peace from this old vicious world.

Reginald: It done dealt you a bad hand, ain't it?

Pause

Leon: *[Crying]* It took my family from me - my wife and my children, all at one time. Didn't even get a chance to tell'em I loved them before they were killed. I told her I would take the bus home, but she insisted on coming to get me. She said that her and the girls had really been missing me while I was away. So they didn't want to wait for the bus to bring me home. They wanted to come get me themselves. My family loved me that way.

Rainey: What happened, Leon?

Leon: The streets were slippery that evening. I reckon it had just stopped raining before she left the house. And it wasn't like Esther to drive when the road was like it was that evening, but I guess she and the girls were

80

eager to see me. Hell, I was just as earnest to see them. I had been away in Korea for four years fulfilling the deeds of the U.S. Military, so I especially longed for the embrace of my family. Called home as soon as I reached the bus station. When Esther picked up on the other end, I say, "The United States done returned your man in one piece". She laughed and rushed off the phone. Packed the girls in the car and took off down the street. Well, apparently she tried to switch lanes too fast and the automobile spun out of control – spun right off the road – right into the side of a building. I sat at that bus station for over an hour waiting on them. We didn't live but twenty blocks away or so from the Greyhound. Normally, it took less than fifteen minutes to get there. So I figured maybe they were just running late. I didn't know, so I just started walking, thinking that maybe I'd run into them on the road. When I got a few blocks away from the station I seen an automobile sitting on fire. Looked like it had been burning for hours. All you could see was the frame of the car, and after the fire engine pulled up and hosed it down I noticed – I noticed that it was my license plate on that automobile. That was my automobile sitting on fire – with my family inside. Wasn't even two hours before I got off the phone with her. I lost everything I loved in a matter of two hours.

Reginald: I know it's tough, son. I've been there. But shooting him ain't gonna make things no easier on you. It definitely ain't gonna bring your family back from the dead.

Leon: Then I'll lay dead with'em.

Leon turns the gun on himself.

Reginald: *[Abruptly]* Now, hold on son! You don't wanna do that. Yeah, it's an easy way out, but it's cowardly. That's the move you've been designed to make, whether it be to take the life of another man, or your own. And it's just like the world to deal you a bad set of cards and expect you to compete in this game of life with the best of them. But that's just how callous it is. And all the while you playing from that raggedy deck of cards you were dealt, the dealer is choking the life from ya, yelling "Focus or Fold – Focus or Fold!" But the problem is you can't think clearly cause you so filled with rage, and your better judgment is clouded in liquor. Hell, ain't nothing wrong with being angry over everything you've lost, but you've been concealing it all the wrong way. *[pause]* But somehow you got to regain your focus, son, cause I ain't gonna let you fold. Now, give me the gun. *[Reginald slowly takes the gun from Leon's hand. Leon breaks down in tears. He begins to swing his fists through the air]*. That's right! Give that world a good ass whipping! There you go – right and a left – left and a right! Hit'em with an uppercut! Stop toying with'em now! Knock'em out!

Reginald pulls out his harmonica and begins to play for the duration of Leon's fit. He swings himself into exhaustion and slumps to the ground weeping.

Brief silence.

Joe: *[Somber]* It was rightly intended for the well-being of folks – but when it became the root of our sustenance, it became a cancer...

Rainey: What's that you talking about, Joe?

Joe: What a fool I've become.

Joe looks around the place, now realizing that the establishment he built for the well-being of his customer's, has in fact become a detriment to those within his community, Leon in particular. Suddenly, Joe grabs his bat and begins to hit the bar counter. He breaks bottles, flips chairs and tables until he wears himself out. The men stand in silence as they observe the wreckage. Moments later, Rashied enters.

Rashied: *[Concerned]* What happened here brotha's? *[Kenny removes his smock and takes the keys from his pocket and places them on the bar counter. He grabs his college catalog and starts to the door]*. What's going on, Kenny?

Pause

Kenny: A conversion is what you call it, ain't it?

Kenny exits. Rashied continues to marvel at the place.

Joe: What the hell you standing there for!

Rashied: Just admiring the beauty of deliverance is all.

Joe: *[Explosive]* Boy, get the hell out of here! *[Joe starts after Rashied]* I said get your ass out of here!

Rashied exits. Everyone's attention is suddenly drawn to the event outside the window. They all move closer to get a better look.

Reginald: Well, I be damned. I can finally see the end of that line.

Rainey: Seem like they all gonna be able to get in there before the office close.

Reginald: Sure seems that way, don't it?

They continue to stare through the window.

Lights go down.

The End

www.ingramcontent.com/pod-product-compliance
Lightning Source LLC
LaVergne TN
LVHW021543080426
835509LV00019B/2800